Vroom!
Corvette

by Mari Schuh

Bullfrog Books

Ideas for Parents and Teachers

Bullfrog Books let children practice reading informational text at the earliest reading levels. Repetition, familiar words, and photo labels support early readers.

Before Reading

- Discuss the cover photo. What does it tell them?
- Look at the picture glossary together. Read and discuss the words.

During Reading

- "Walk" through the book with the reader. Discuss new or unfamiliar words. Sound them out together.
- Look at the photos together. Point out the photo labels.

After Reading

- Prompt the child to think more. Ask: Have you seen a Corvette? What color was it?

Bullfrog Books are published by Jump!
3500 American Blvd W, Suite 150
Bloomington, MN 55431
www.jumplibrary.com

Copyright © 2026 Jump! International copyright reserved in all countries. No part of this book may be reproduced in any form without written permission from the publisher.

Jump! is a division of FlutterBee Education Group.

Library of Congress Cataloging-in-Publication Data

Names: Schuh, Mari C., 1975- author.
Title: Corvette / by Mari Schuh.
Description: Minneapolis, MN: Jump!, Inc., [2026]
Series: Vroom! | Includes index.
Audience: Ages 5–8
Identifiers: LCCN 2024054477 (print)
LCCN 2024054478 (ebook)
ISBN 9798896620143 (hardcover)
ISBN 9798896620150 (paperback)
ISBN 9798896620167 (ebook)
Subjects: LCSH: Corvette automobile—Juvenile literature.
Classification: LCC TL215.C6 S385 2026 (print)
LCC TL215.C6 (ebook)
DDC 629.222/2—dc23/eng/20250210
LC record available at https://lccn.loc.gov/2024054477
LC ebook record available at https://lccn.loc.gov/2024054478

Editor: Jenna Gleisner
Designer: Anna Peterson

Photo Credits: DarthArt/iStock, cover; JoshBryan/Shutterstock, 1; PaulLP/Shutterstock, 3; Brandon Woyshnis/iStock, 4, 23br; Brandon Woyshnis/Shutterstock, 5, 20–21; Paul Pollock/iStock, 6–7; Luke Sharrett/Bloomberg/Getty, 8–9; Martina Birnbaum/Shutterstock, 10–11; Wirestock/Dreamstime, 12, 13; jeanpierre/Adobe Stock, 14–15, 23tl, 23bl; Darren Brode/Shutterstock, 16, 23bm, 24; Ron Adar/Shutterstock, 17, 23tr; Arpad Benedek/Alamy, 18–19, 23tm; Vehicles/Alamy, 22.

Printed in the United States of America at Corporate Graphics in North Mankato, Minnesota.

Table of Contents

Fast Cars	4
Parts of a Corvette	22
Picture Glossary	23
Index	24
To Learn More	24

Corvette
(kor-VET)

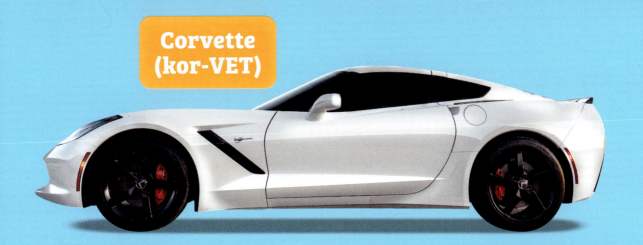

Fast Cars

Vroom!

A **sports car** drives by.

It is a Corvette.

The first one was made in Michigan.

That was in 1953.

Michigan

Now they are made in Kentucky.

Cool!

Most have two doors.

They have only two seats.

This one is low.

It is close to the ground.

It races!

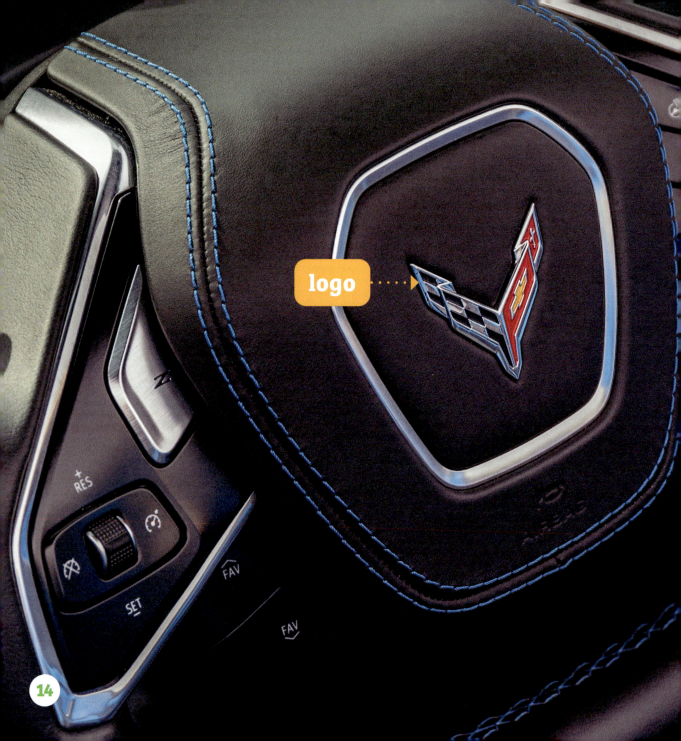

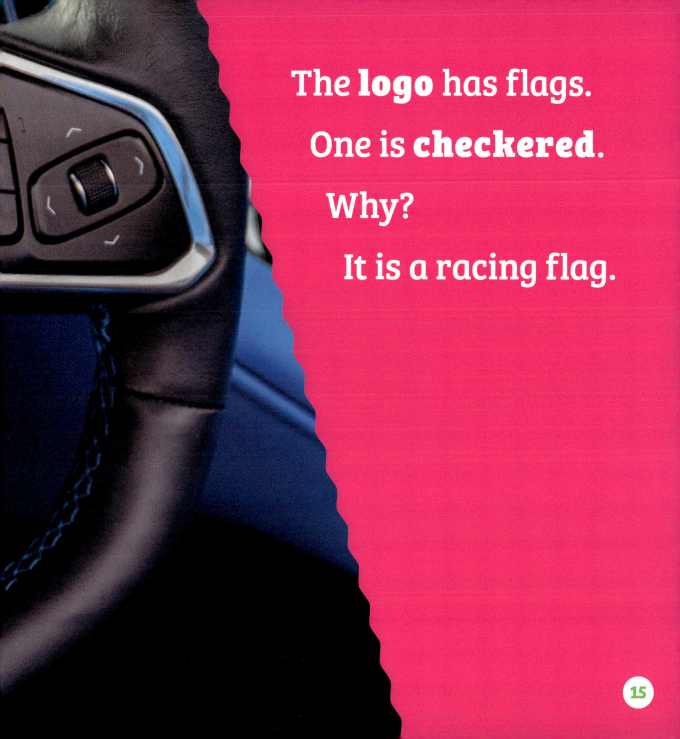

The **logo** has flags.
One is **checkered**.
Why?
It is a racing flag.

There are many **models**.
One is the Stingray.

The E-Ray is a **hybrid**.

This is a C8.

Its **engine** is in a new spot.

Where?

It is behind the seats.

It is a sunny day.

Put the roof down.

Let's go!

Parts of a Corvette

A 2025 Corvette ZR1 can go 233 miles (375 kilometers) per hour! Take a look at the parts of a Corvette!

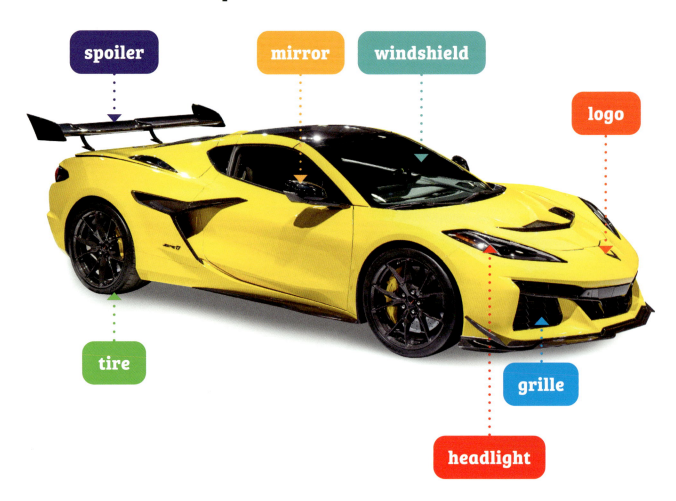

Picture Glossary

checkered
Having a pattern of squares that goes back and forth between two colors.

engine
A machine that makes something move by using gasoline or another energy source.

hybrid
Using electricity and gasoline for power.

logo
A symbol that stands for a company.

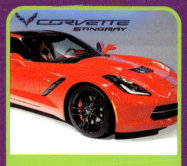

models
Particular types or designs.

sports car
A car that is made to go fast and handle turns well.

Index

C8 18
doors 11
engine 18
E-Ray 17
hybrid 17
Kentucky 8
logo 15
Michigan 7
races 13
roof 21
seats 11, 18
Stingray 16

To Learn More

Finding more information is as easy as 1, 2, 3.

❶ Go to **www.factsurfer.com**

❷ Enter **"Corvette"** into the search box.

❸ Choose your book to see a list of websites.